I Am Sitting
On My Glasses

by

Lois Anderson Leister

Bloomington, IN   authorHOUSE®   Milton Keynes, UK

AuthorHouse™
1663 Liberty Drive, Suite 200
Bloomington, IN 47403
www.authorhouse.com
Phone: 1-800-839-8640

AuthorHouse™ UK Ltd.
500 Avebury Boulevard
Central Milton Keynes, MK9 2BE
www.authorhouse.co.uk
Phone: 08001974150

© 2006 Lois Anderson Leister. All rights reserved.

No part of this book may be reproduced, stored in a retrieval system, or transmitted by any means without the written permission of the author.

First published by AuthorHouse 9/7/2006

ISBN: 1-4259-5500-2 (sc)

Printed in the United States of America
Bloomington, Indiana

This book is printed on acid-free paper.

Dedication

This book is dedicated to
my dear sisters, Marie and Melba
and to Chaplains Ray, Vernon and
Bob at Menno Haven.

Table of Contents

LIFE LINES   43

LOVE LINES   73

LAUGH LINES

I Am Sitting On My Glasses

I am sitting on my glasses,
I have done it twice before;
I wish I could remember
not to do it anymore.

Sometimes I finish reading
and put them on a chair
or up above my forehead
and forget I put them there.

Where did I put my car keys?
I will look for them, you know,
as soon as I remember
where it is I need to go.

Oh yes, now it comes back to me;
my brains have come unmixed.
When I get off my glasses
I must go and get them fixed.

When I Am Old

When I am old, that is to say,
when hair, now salt-and-pepper gray,
has turned snow white I have a plan.
With no more seasons to delay,
to find myself a laughing man.

Perhaps he'll sport a bit of tan,
an outdoor man would suit me fine,
one who will love me if he can.
A dancing man would be divine,
if he can stay awake past nine.

Perhaps, if he can pass the test,
I'll ply him with a little wine,
and we will flee our wintry nest
to head down south. I have a zest
for gypsy living in Key West,
for gypsy living in Key West.

An Excess of Affection

He gazed upon me soulfully
from limpid pools of brown;
I could tell that he was panting
as he eyed me up and down.
Then he leaped upon me,
and I struggled to get up.
If he does that one more time,
I'll give away that pup.

Lois Anderson Leister

Feeding the Human Animal

Sam can't rise if he kneels to pray.
His body cast gets in the way.
I can't fold my hands today
because my shoulder's gone astray.
But when I stumble to my bed
to rest my white and weary head,
I'll know at least when all is said,
an orthopedist has been fed.

We're Camping!

The kids say, "Are we almost there?"
The dog wants out, the headlights glare.
It looks like rain but I don't care.
We're camping!

The rain starts as we reach the site;
we're setting up without a light.
I left it home, but that's all right.
We're camping!

We set the jacks, the level's right.
We plug in. Now we have a light
to cheer us through the rainy night.
We're camping!

I just turned on the TV set;
the lights went out, my feet are wet,
but folks, you ain't seen nothing' yet.
We're camping!

Site Scene

In every camp there is a site
bisected by a path,
halfway from the faucet,
halfway to the bath.
And every camper has at hand
one necessity
except the luckless middle-man
who usually is me.

Camping Vacation
(Don't Forget to Write)

Dear Grandmother, first day went fine,
except it rained at half-past nine,
and ten, and two. At half-past four
the rain swelled shut the restroom door.

The second day was better and
we did much more than we had planned
by hiking every trail that day
in search of Joe who ran away.

The third day—Well, I can't complain;
no one got lost, it didn't rain.
But Johnny broke his little toe,
tripped on a stake that didn't show.

But still our spirits soar on high,
Hooray for camping is our cry
despite the grace my verses lack,
written while flat upon my back.

Try It, You'll Like It

Off to the moon! It's a great place to go.
The campground's the latest one yet.
It has only been used by a few men, you know,
so think of the welcome you'd get.

You can walk on the moon on the tips of your toes,
and leap halfway up to the stars.
You won't be distracted by smog in the nose,
or the noises of busses and cars.

The litter is light; it has all been confined
to a place called Tranquility Sea.
So why don't you take all your buddies along
before they start charging a fee.

But if while exploring the weird lunar light,
you should worry about me and peek,
you will find me on earth pitching camp on a site,
I couldn't get into last week.

Podiatry

I trusted him that fateful night,
assured that he would treat me right.
His hands were gentle on my skin,
(But then, that's how they all begin.)
Today, with energies deplete,
I cannot rise upon my feet,
but lie upon a couch of pain
and curse the man, with outraged brain,
who took a scalpel yesterday
and whittled part of my sole away.

Leister Parade

My husband walks so close behind
he stomps me if I dawdle,
and to my sudden burst of speed
responds with frantic waddle.

Folks whisper, "If he were a man
he'd stand his ground and clip her."
But my uncompromising back
hides his broken zipper.

They Forgot

A warm flood carried through my dreams until
the frigid air yanked me from sleep;
I was too cold to rise and leave the wet.
My sister lay beside me, boneless, warm.
Now I, who always scorned a hug,
squirmed close against the dryness of her side.

From sodden misery I weighed my plight;
A warm dry shore lay at her other side.
Shivering, I crawled from clinging sheets.
to creep across her body. "Move over,"
I said, and shoved her toward the wet.

"MAMA!" came the indignant cry, "MAMA!"
"Shh!" I said. "Mama's asleep."
Mama's no-nonsense voice was not asleep.
It called across the night,
"What is it, Girls?"

They saw my chilly plight, but they forgot;
Sister, father, mother, all forgot
I was the "precious baby" of the house.

Wearing The Holter Monitor

I do not mind the monitor
encircling my waist,
though I can think of ways
to be more happily embraced.
I suffer the indignity
of going to the john
while being monitored,
although my privacy is gone.
But I deplore the fact that sex
is robbed of its attraction,
if I must take a little book,
and catalogue the action.

Curious Phenomenon

The caveman wore his tresses long
courting a mate in fur sarong,
a fact that makes me ponder.
Men wear hair short
when women sport
a length of which I'm fonder.
But history repeats, they say,
and while the mini-skirts today,
are going up to yonder,
the more anatomy left bare,
the more men hide their eyes in hair.

Lamentable Quotes

"You can if you think you can."
They said. "Try, try again."
"The game isn't lost till the whistle blows."
"Keep keeping on." But then,
"There are always two sides to every coin."
I quote with proverbial rue.
"Don't think about it, just do it." they said.
And I'm who he did it to.

No Allowance for Aging

The world has not stopped singing as it spins.
The earth still flings a fragrance from its pores
to celebrate the spring. And I still celebrate
the spring, the earth and even handsome men.

Mechanically Speaking

I view my gear box with suspicion;
one early robin flits a wing,
and, prematurely, my transmission
shifts automatically to spring.

Limerick

Have you heard about Edna and Fred?
They were eighty the day they were wed.
They went to Niagara,
and both took Viagra,
and died with a smile in their bed.

KID STUFF

Neonatal

Soon they will say, "You have a child."
but I have known you all these months.
I cherished you, and nourished you.
I soothed you when you leaped within me.
and prayed for you when the pains came early.
and I have not forgotten all the years
I ached because you were not with me.
Beloved unborn child, soon I shall see your face.

After Birth

A tear away from weeping
and just behind a smile,
too clean and soft for sleeping,
I'll simply glow awhile
to glory in the wonder
and beauty of my yield.
The world hangs suspended,
I am fulfilled.

To Whom It May Concern
(Baby IV)

It is much too soon to cast my news
to the pros and cons of public views.
This is a private invitation
for you to share with me
the love and joy and wonder
of my new pregnancy.

Baby V

Too many children gossipers will say,
but Baby Five, if you could hear the way
my heart is singing, how your birth
has sent my spirits winging,
Beloved One, my every breath
thanks God for you this day.

Five Times Love

Five times love is heart's arithmetic.
Although I cannot total up the score
of even one times love,
I do know this, five times love is more.
Love cannot be measured out or split;
this share for you, for you another part.
God designed, each child has all of it,
five times heart.

Little Girl's Face

You know that I could never paint.
So clumsy with a brush
that on a canvas all my oils
turn to a slimy mush.
But last night on a pillow
framed by silken, shiny hair,
her face all soft with soap and love,
my daughter lay, and where
a painter would use oils, my heart
captured a portrait there.

Little Boy's Face

If words could paint a portrait of my son,
I'd say, "his hair is yellow-brown
with twists and turns that won't lie down.
His eyes are blue but you hardly see
the color that they chanced to be
for the laughter that they cast about,
or grief when tears come tumbling out.
His lips can quiver and tremble and fall
till your heart sinks within you. And yet, best of all,
they can turn into laughter and sunshine and song
that brightens the world like a rainbow or dawn."

Lois Anderson Leister

Shadow Figure

I have a little shadow
that pursues me room to room.
When I bend to pick up toys,
she clouts me with my broom.
After I have swept the floor
she overturns the trash.
The pail that holds scrub water
is designed for her to splash.
And if this ending seems abrupt
be tolerant with me;
I have a little shadow
climbing on my knee.

Victim

Joseph climbed out of his crib today
and fell with a crash to the floor.
While I was soothing his pride and a lump,
Johnny colored a door.

Joseph emptied the hamper
and locked himself in a room.
Johnny broke the bristles
out of a brand-new broom.

Then they found the laundry
folded neat and square
and, giggling ecstatically,
threw clean clothes everywhere.

I was ready to scold and spank
pint and half-pint size,
but melted in the warm blue gaze
of four I-love-you eyes.

The Dilemma

Dear Lord, I hate to call on you
for such a little task.
With all the big things you must do,
I feel a fool to ask.
But, Johnny has Cub Scouts till six.
(Bedtime is half-past eight.)
If you could save us from this fix
it really would be great.
Today is Nancy's birthday
so I said that we could eat
a pizza out at Shakey's
as a sort of birthday treat.
We could do everything with ease
if you would set it right.
O Lord, don't let the teachers give us
homework for tonight.

Plea

Someday I must renounce my magic place,
perhaps a bone my kisses cannot knit,
or hurts my blowing on cannot erase
will childhood part to show the truth of it.

When I stand naked of my godly guise,
bereft of any elevating grace,
dear child, look beyond your vast surprise
and settle for the love upon my face.

Little Boys

Three sons the Lord has given me,
I, who am so unknowing.
The youngest in a field of girls,
I never saw one growing.

My grubby, noisy, little boys
scorn the things I yearn,
yet hold me captive for an hour
at how their cowlicks turn.

Girls are clean and soft and sweet
and patient in their waiting
but, O my darling little boys,
I find you captivating.

Routine Monday

Tissue stuck to corduroy,
white lint on darkest green,
pebbles, bottle caps and nails
clank in the machine.

Bits of gaily colored cloth
that fade a ghastly hue,
bees and string and butterflies,
worms and beetles too.

I can rewash the corduroy,
replace the worn machine,
bleach the faded clothing,
and make it almost clean,

but I cannot deny my boy
the greatest of his pleasures.
Why else are pockets put in pants
except to hold his treasures?

Foster Child

You are the prayer I say each night,
a silent tear when the dark grows long.
You are a giggle of delight,
an oft repeated nursery song.
You are a hurt that won't let go.
The memories I must review
when least expected go to show
my constant, aching love for you.
My only solace is the thought,
though miles separate us far,
my prayers and tears will be for aught,
if you but know how loved you are.

After

After the hurried hubbub of the dawn
when sleepy children strain reluctant lids
and burrow deeply into warm cocoons,
after they gulp their cereal and juice,
and panic-stricken, search for mislaid books,
clanging lunch pails, calling loud goodbyes
flavored by jelly kisses, after the banging door,
silence drops a blanket over echoes.
The mind now free, opens
to silence, a morning glory
beginning soft communion with the day.

Graduation

Love should not be a burden,
a fetter or a strain
that one must carry heavily
as duty or a chain.
So swing your slender shoulders free;
I open wide the door.
In waving you beyond my reach,
I could not love you more.

Kathy

Beloved daughter, caught behind shy walls
identical to mine, we stand apart
aching in twin reserves that only
in bright moments briefly crumble.
But we are blessed, each with a gift of pen,
so I receive letters that wing your love
across tongue barriers and soaring walls,
I translate love to poetry for you.

Lois Anderson Leister

The First Time – The Worst Time

My hindsight tells me now that I
should not have let him go.
I longed to keep him here with me,
but feared to let him know.

If he would just come back right now,
I would be so blasé
he would not think I noticed
that he had been away.

This surely is the longest day
that I have lived so far.
My son is driving solo
in the family's only car.

Grown Son

Where is the boy of yesterday,
the boy he used to be,
who never seemed to mind a fall,
that froze the blood in me.

Once he found a lizard
he cared for every day;
it rode upon his shoulder
as though satisfied to stay.

Today my boy, a mustached man,
has babies on his knee.
I love the man, but oh I miss
the boy he used to be.

First Born

She came today, first born and longest from the nest.
I tried to think when she had come alone,
without a child or husband, sometimes both.
What would we talk about? Would words
run down like dying breaths, or spurt
in stilted phrases awkward to the tongue?
Did she think important thoughts
had been too long unspoken? Had she found
another ear that served better than mine?
Was love a crumbling bridge so poorly tended
that words could not reach out across the span?
She came in quiet wisdom, knowing a lifetime
shared and fed by love and not erased by time.

LIFE LINES

Dreams

My dreams are lifted upward to the sky.
In glowing arches, gracefully they bend
to change their hue as quickly as a sigh
with colors fading softly near the end.
But while they live they form a lovely hue
where yellows, reds, and shades of purple blend.
Old dreams are like old fires, softly blue.
They warm the wistful corners the heart
while minds are lifted onward to pursue
new dreams that random winds may blow apart.
But dreams are lovely, whether new or old,
and worth pursuing from the very start.
The glowing rainbow makes our dreaming bold,
and needs no promise of a pot of gold.

Lois Anderson Leister

Nightmares

It will not be today I lose my mind.
I can hold on, get through, and still survive.
It will not be tonight if I am spared
nightmares that plunge me down the well again,
where crumbled walls of brick my prison makes.
A hint of light triangles from the rim;
it tries to penetrate the dims of mist,
and fails. This time, perhaps the two who
chat above will stay to heed my cry.
Perhaps the dust clouds will not leave the walls
and fill my mouth and nose to strangle me.
And if I breathe again, perhaps the two
will not desert me, voices echoed back.
Perhaps this time I will not lift my face
to choke and call again through dust and tears.

Undone and Never Spoken

Death sends no surgeon to attend
to the survivor's need.
We plunge the blade into our wounds
and suicidal, bleed
for what we should have said or done,
writhing excruciate,
impaled upon an epitaph,
Too little and too late.

Childhood Reunion

The rope swing in the apple tree is dusty from disuse.
The pathway to my secret place, lacking foot abuse,
is wild with vine; ivy and thorn
grow where I tasted the dew of the morn
with bare, searching toes.
Here the snows
packed, protected from the sun,
the last soggy patches to rivulets run.
I painted my visions here, reshaped my dreams
to the shape of my growing. How recent it seems.
Time has forgotten that young and forlorn,
a child died here when a woman was born.

Contemplation

Today my words walked softly,
not to tread on bare-toed feelings.
I hunted kinder no's, found fewer uses for them.
When bright enthusiasm cried,
"Say Mom, I have a idea."
I found the time to listen.
I did not mind picking up toys today.
A little boy who lived next door is dead.

The Letter

I reached the mailbox by the wall
before the postman came
and climbed above a flowered bank
to let the crab grass claim
my presence and permit me watch
an hour the empty road.
Upon a car that wasn't there,
I felt my eyes explode.
But when the engine neared my box,
I let it idle by
intent upon offending weeds,
I could not spare my eye.
Reluctantly I lifted up
to leave the flower bed,
stiff beneath the weight of hope
that trembled on a thread.
I pushed my footsteps to the box,
braced to meet the pain
that, if my letter had not come,
must shatter me again.

The Road To Yesterday

It slid beneath a barnyard gate
to curve its way from door to door
in country miles across the state,
a kinship track upon the floor
of this great earth. When sadness came
the people built a house of God
along the road, and in His name
bequeathed a bit of holy sod
where their beloved dead might lie
together near his trusted hand.
And as the hard years hurried by,
they put down roots into the land.

Then roads that wound from town to town
became gray ribbons of cement
for men who needed more than brown
to link a mighty continent.
Yet when man pulls his roots to roam
an ocean or a city street,
a velvet ribbon pulls him home
to feel brown earth beneath his feet.

School Crossing

They bunch up near his corner, two in front.
She, a thin straight line wearing
authority like a crown. Brown and bold from
summer, the scowling boy will challenge her,
nudge her from power. She will give way
with haughty unconcern, but not today.
The big policeman smiles.
He stiffs his arm and faces north
to hold back traffic with an open palm.
They cross under the outstretched arm,
some with shy smiles. Others pretend
he is not there. He changes corners,
pirouettes on booted cat's feet.
Some unwritten law decrees that children
cross behind him now, all but the one,
the little one who plays London Bridge
beneath his arm with brown braids dancing.
His fingers smooth the air above the woven hair,
not touching. Time shimmers in sunlight,
falls away, and he is ten years old, tasting
sun-hot streets with summer feet.

Giants

No broken bones; no blackened eyes.
He opened doors and held her chair,
and walked beside her near the curb,
and he was loud in praise to all their friends.
She was his life, his love, his everything.
He would not want to live if she were gone.
When they went home, he let her pass
before him going in and barred the door.

Then he released the giants,
towering, raging giants,
to gouge huge chunks of sunlight
from her soul.

Offering

I have a door that only opens in
and am condemned to waiting
hopefully, unable to begin
to swing it wide. Tied by hesitating
I place my door shyly
where you may see. If you
touch your hand upon the grating,
you may open me.

One Silent Moment

From wistful, lonely corridors
souls, outstretched, are reaching
through nebulae of mustn't-touch,
welcoming, beseeching.
Answers hover in the space
where eyes unite in shouting.
Then worlds intrude and questioners
return to dreams and doubting.

Old Battlefields

Whispery illusions rise from coffin trenches.
Grasses sway uncrushed, unnoticing
beneath the weightless feet.
Surging waves of dusty blue, dim gray,
writhe in death contortions.

Too much of life and flesh, I seem
obscene among the bloodless dead.
Hesitant, I start across the field,
but my reluctant faltering desecrates,
and wave on wave, the whispery illusions
fall back into their coffin trenches.

Renegade

Don't fence me in by tired little things
like lunch served exactly at noon each day.
I must chase fog fingers, count moon rings.
Call me home, but teach me first the way
to catch my spirit which with such agility
eludes the harness of respectability.

Season Reasoning

Sister was born in March and yet
is soft and summer slow,
slipping toward maturity
like the autumn glow.

In October, I was born,
yet I am like the spring,
leaping and loud with laughter
and sudden happening.

I think it was quite nice of God
though I don't know his reason,
to disregard the calendar
and bloom us out of season.

Birth Of A Poem

Poised on a precipice of mind,
above a plunging cataract
of thought, a revelation
quivers, half minded
to slip quietly
unrecognized,
back to oblivion.

Empathy

I have known enough of private hells,
of bitterness and ashes
and gray thought islands.
When I see the bleakness in your eyes
I long to reach to you,
to touch, and hold,
and turn your thoughts
to make you young again.

Without Regret

I am glad I am no longer young
with heart so new and yearning
that one soft love song sweetly sung
brings tears, a finger's touch so burning
it leaves me all undone,
glad there is no returning.
I could not abide the pain
so all-exposed, growing up again.

Hope

Spring, come over that bleakest peak
and spread your velvet down.
The earth is tired of the cold
and weary of the brown.

I have been full of winter,
so many seasons straight.
My heart is blighted with the frost
and ponderous of gait.

But when you rise on yonder peak
and paint the valley green,
I will be warm as laughter;
I will be young as spring.

So Late So Early

It seems unreal that I will not remain
suspended between youth and age.
I have traveled close enough to see
that death will reach its hand and I
will be unable to ignore its touch.
Perhaps I will not mind. I know God, and I know
that joy undreamed awaits beyond this life.
But I would wait awhile. I have not pried
the meaning of myself out of my bones.
I would wait until the ones I love
no longer haunt me with their needs.
I hope I do not die with protests on my lips,
forgetting that I once hungered for God,
and search for further reasons to delay.

Shining Roads

The hills of home are calling me
like homing bird or woodland thing
across the miles of misery
to stir a heart that ceased to sing.

I long to run from shades of pain,
to lick my wounds and cool my brow,
to travel back the twisted lane
stretching from yesterday to now.
Somewhere along that tortured way
small bits of life still stand and wait,
the roads not chosen yesterday,
shining and inviolate.

Thus Came Man

Man's mind, soaring eternity and space,
converts dreams to reality, extends
vision three-hundred-thousand miles,
and wings an utterance across a galaxy.
Spellbound upon a waiting earth, we trace
man movements in a lunar wilderness.
Incomprehensible this miracle until,
meaningful as breath, we see
half an inch of footprints in the dust.

The Sparrow

A bird stood pensive on the grass;
he looked to left and right.
On either side brick buildings stood
and limited his sight.
He turned his vision upward
to the narrow strip of sky
and felt oppressed and smothered.
How like that bird am I.

A Touch of the Wand

I wish that all the world could see
the maple as it looks to me,
fired with glory, crimson crowned,
that all the world hear the sound
of laughter dancing in my breast
through simple words. It is a test
of all that I will ever be,
and nothing if not poetry.

Lois Anderson Leister

The World of Pre-Dawn

Pursuing sleep across my mind
with shadow logic far surpassing
step-by-step realistic sequence,
dreams transport me, all absorbing,
summon undilute emotions,
unconditioned pure reactions,
capture me and plummet onward,
skidding to a sudden standstill
on the precipice of waking.
At one penetrating pinprick,
suddenly disintegrating

Flight To Sanctuary

Somewhere, over a distant hill,
a moonlit acre lies circled by
dark anonymous trees, where I
cast off the human bonds of duty
and expected patterns to flee
secretly, without a light. There
I fling myself upon the slope to feel
stiff hill grass spring against my cheek.
I lie penitent and after patient waiting,
earth absorbs my hastening,
exchanging it for her tranquility.

The Cure

If laughter were dispensed for pain
across the counter of a store,
some hurts would disappear like rain
when droplets meet a desert floor.
It would not go against the grain
to try to laugh a little more.

I wonder, should I tell you more?
There is no cure-all for the pain,
but if we harvest laughter's grain,
or buy it from a laughter store,
and heap it golden on the floor,
we could get through a siege of rain.

I think on days when spirits rain,
we need some laughter even more.
When hope sags lifeless on the floor,
and fails the bravest soul in pain,
I'd hurry to the nearest store
for baskets full of such a grain.

If I could grow this magic grain
I'd shower it in rainbow rain
upon the shattered. I would store
enough for ten or maybe more
to share with souls beset by pain,
and stack it on my silo floor.
When it was gone, I'd sweep the floor;
to sift the chaff for one last grain
to dull the edge of someone's pain.
Sometimes a soul has too much rain,
so I must push a little more
for buying laughter from a store.

To purchase laughter in a store,
I'd take my soapbox to the floor
of Congress and say even more.
We need a stock of magic grain
to bless us with its golden rain
and be an antidote for pain.

When hearts have pain, sometimes they store
the drowning rain. I take the floor
for laughter's grain. It serves us more.

Time

When I turn back memory,
I see the girl I used to be
running barefoot down the lane,
sun-brown and young and wild and free.
She sings of love, a sweet refrain,
a joyful sound she can't restrain.
She does not know of misery
and is a stranger yet to pain.

But I am old and smaller now
and bending like a fruited bough.
There's not a thing that I can gain
except more wrinkles on my brow.
But I can bear and not complain,
and flourish on a higher plane,
to be as much as I can be
until at last time stops for me.

LOVE LINES

Kisses In His Eyes

He said goodbye with kisses in his eyes,
while in his chest a lonely silence thundered,
Don't go, stay here with me!
Clutching his words, "Have fun and win a prize",
I stumbled through the barrier where
silver wings would soar the clouds
and carry me to meet my dreams.
The hurried faceless crowds were not
as real as thundered silence, not as real
as kisses in his eyes.

A Touch of Splendor

If I have loved you it has been as one
who comes from God as healer of my pain,
to set aside, your special purpose done,
unless the torture rack should twist again.
If I have loved you it has been as friend
through times of trust and gentle nurturing,
a pleasant comfort destined to extend
sure and unchanging, to that final spring.
If I have loved you it has been as faint
as color pencil sketches on a wall.
Etching it here today in poet paint,
perhaps I should not call it love at all.
And yet it is unique. It stands apart
and brings a touch of splendor to my heart.

Thank You, Friend

Thank you friend, for recognizing needs
that I concealed behind a wall of lies.
Thank you for weeping when you saw me bleed
after I stripped myself of all disguise.

Thank you for trusting me and giving voice
to pain you never dared express before.
I will not give you cause to rue the choice.
I'll shelter you with silence evermore.

But most of all, now that you see me plain,
My failures, flaws, and weaknesses in view,
Thank you for showing me that I remain
precious, respected, and still loved by you.

Quarter-Century Plant

When I first blossomed into love,
I did not know how rare my flowering.
I only knew the brightness died
and all my petals folded.

The seasons passed and I remained
untouched and never opened
until you came. Now, I am
a quarter-century plant blooming.

Across The Room

Perhaps I turned too soon, or you too late,
our timing off a fraction of a minute.
My heart lurched with an unexpected weight
that seemed to have a touch of sadness in it,
a sense of loss more wistful than a sigh,
because our eyes had failed to kiss goodbye.

Lois Anderson Leister

No Strings Attached

If at last there is a time
you do not ring my phone
or move against my shoulder,
if warmth deserts your tone,
perhaps I'll say, "Good riddance!"
and smile and let you go.
But if I cry myself to sleep
at night you will not know.
It is my gentle offering
that should love lose its glow,
I will not try to cling to you,
but softly let you go.

Roller Coaster

You were with me on the steepest climb,
the endless falls, the sharpest curves.
When I was reeling, you were there,
a god-man answering my needs.

But I am stronger now.
Perhaps—well, just perhaps,
I can ride and rise and fall alone.
Perhaps, glad that I set you free,
I'll climb the air alone with God.

This time, reaching the sky's blind edge,
I may not hurtle down to dark despair.
This time I may not need your hand.
But if I fall, will you reach out once more
to hold me fast?

If Wishes Were. . .

I would go with you in muted hours
when twilight rain falls softly on the earth
to crouch in silence waiting for the first
deer sentinel to glide into the glen.

I would search for draba at your side,
kneeling in April earth with gentle hands
to push aside the overgrowth and find
the wonder of a tiny wool-leaved plant.

I would share your secret world with you,
not as a stranger, not an alien.
I am twilight, mist and solitude.
I have a kinship with the earth and you.

Before You Leave Me

My eyes seek yours.
Touching you like blind hands,
I drink in nourishment for my soul.
I store up memories
against the time of famine
when I do not see your face.

Your Step

You hesitate before my door
and my heart stumbles, loses step.
My breathing feathers.
I command my heart to slow
and hope you do not check my vital signs.
I swear my eyes to silence
before they shout my joy at seeing you.

The Path

You have worn a path between my heart and mind.
By day you dart through wordless thoughts,
quicksilvering the sun in beams of light
brief as a breath, no longer than your name.

Sometimes you slip the shaded paths of night
with gifts of memories beneath your arms;
I unwrap them slowly one by one
to fold, soft as a smile, around my heart.

But when you walk the vapor mist of dreams
to drift the path between me and the dawn
with empty, wistful, might-have-beens,
your path becomes a spillway for my tears.

Tentative

My soul, with boldness, always has
charted its course before,
but now approaches quietly
and softly taps your door.
Our friendship, newly reaching out,
fragile as a wing,
awes me by its capacity
to be a mighty thing.

Parting

I know that all of life is change;
hearts don't break with pain;
it is right that some must leave
while others must remain.

Bur right is comfortless to me;
cold logic holds no charms;
wisdom can't reach out to touch
and hold me in its arms.

And it is rare when two can share
their thoughts and dreams and scars,
and know that sharing any more
would take them to the stars.

Flowers

Love can be a vine, encircling, clinging,
not content to circle once,
but many times entwining.
My love is not a vine. It does not cling;
it blossoms flower-like with cherishing,
and given nourishment lives to eternity.
But in the touch of an uncaring hand,
it folds to nothingness.
If you should cease your cherishing,
my love will not pursue;
you will not find me clinging.
Flowers die so quietly.

The Words Not Spoken

Someone I loved is dead today
and all the times I did not say
I love you press upon my brow
edging my grief with torment now.
I loved him and in grief's cold clutch,
no spoken words could hurt so much.

Extrasensory

You call to me across the miles
without an aid of man's design.
No email, telephone, or pen
enlightens me. No outward sign
from you explains how I receive
your every reaching thought and need.
But should a blade pierce through your heart,
my own would split apart and bleed.

Tonight

You are not content tonight
to wait for quiet moments in my heart.
Your presence reigns unchallenged over me.
My actions are a pantomime my shell performs,
acceptable, routine, while underneath, I breathe
with you, and ache, and call your name.

Lois Anderson Leister

ESP

I feel you lifting me
out of my written words,
feel you stir to this new personality.
You stand before the door
imagining my inner room.

Your privacy is an illusion.
Unaware that I can see,
You loose your fantasies.
Together we romp unfettered
through your brain.

Bilingual

It is difficult to answer, facing you.
The words you speak are not the words
your eyes are shouting.
My mind falters, yielding to your eyes,
to urgency that you awaken.
Then I grasp my thoughts and summon words,
communicating in two languages.

Heart Attack

If I drift across your mind
like sunlight, or a prayer
or looking in the mirror,
you find me shadowed there,
know that across the miles my heart,
defying man's convention,
is using woman-witchery
to capture your attention.

My Love For You

My love is made of song and joy.
yet is an anguished thing
that fills me in the sleepless night
with need and hungering.
My love knows triumph that your pulse
is quickened by my touch;
that of a thousand souls, not one
can stir you quite as much.

If you take your love from me
leaving my soul bereft
of all but pain-wracked memories,
I will forgive the theft
and breathe and move and smile and speak.
No one will see the pain,
or that I died of agony
and cannot love again.

Triolet

My life is like a triolet
that keeps repeating you.
I have reason to regret
my life is like a triolet.
Although I struggle to forget
and stray a beat or two,
my life is like a triolet
that keeps repeating you.

Just Once

You healed the wistful wounds left by rejection,
healed with touch what only you could heal,
and for a day and more I was content.
A one-time touch, the only one, you said,
and then you touched your lips to mine. I circle
with my tongue and taste where yours have been.
I cherish what you gave in that brief kiss
to all the secret corners of my soul.

If

When silent silver raindrops bring
bright dandelions to the lawn
and leaf buds open into spring,
I will not see, if love is gone.

But I will know the fragrant earth,
the glory of the skies,
and witness April giving birth
if love is in your eyes.

Love Me Enough

My mind will journey to a land
where words are music, shouting
to be heard. Love me enough
that when I go where you can't follow,
you will not mind or tie me
with resentment. Set me winging free,
I will return bearing my harvest.
Its richness is for you and all
I have to offer. Love me enough.

My Gift To You

I give you little parts of me
to carry in your heart:
Laughter, a dream or poetry,
a moment that may start
like chain reaction, memory
to make your spirit light,
to wrap around you lovingly
and warm you in the night.

Your Note

After the knife had torn its twisted way,
after the flames, neglected, sighed to cinders,
your note came. But pain was more familiar
than your touch, too splintered now for band-aids
to save the fallen warriors of my dreams.

A Kind of Dying

With the first deadly words,
all senses flee in terror from the pain
to wait, breath held, in wretched nothingness
while voice, mechanical, seeks out last proofs.
It cannot risk one dream escaping
that later must be slain.
Wrapped in a Novocain of shock,
animal instinct drags its wounds
into the blank beyond before it flings
itself in wild abandon to its agony.

My Soul

My soul, if you can keep from overflowing
to wail and mourn the anguish of your plight,
perhaps you can survive with no one knowing
the salted flood that drowns you in the night.

But O my soul, you spread in lavish language
your miracle of joy when love was new.
How could you know that loss would fill the last page,
a lightening strike that splintered you in two?

And you are tired now from too much caring,
without resilience left to start again.
I wonder, does a soul collapse with bearing
and crumble into dust from too much pain?

Unguarded

I thought I did so well today.
I left my dreams of you behind
to settle, sort and store away
important matters in my mind.

When I remained aloof, unmoved,
through one long day's eternity,
I told myself that I had proved
you don't mean very much to me.

Then I, unguarded, dropped the bars
and my emotions tumbled through
to shout in anguish to the stars
my hungry, aching love for you.

Vacancy

I have outlived the heartbreak years,
the searing pain of loss and yearning.
At last the sweeping tide of grief
has ebbed and will not be returning.
Where once a face, a voice or laughter
could bring to life the faintest ember,
the very things of no forgetting
no longer pain me to remember.
But having harbored you a guest,
unwelcome, yet a part of me,
there is no joy in emptiness,
it is so lonely being free.

A Thousand Years

After you had gone away,
I gathered up each bit
of me I hadn't shared with you
and made a heap of it.

Poems you never knew I wrote,
I was too shy to show,
a friend or two you hadn't met,
a place we didn't go.

It was the smallest gathering
on which to build again,
there wasn't even half enough
to smother out the pain.

And yet I fought to build a life.
I struggled so to win it,
another time, another place
with other people in it.

But I have learned acceptance now,
a knowledge born of tears.
First love, the uninvited guest,
stays a thousand years

I Know

If there is one thing certain that I know
it is that hearts don't really break with pain.
Instead, they swell to bursting with the strain
of memories that flow like waterfalls
in circled eddies where the undertow
is fed by flooding freshets from the brain
They surge with grief, but still the heart remains
battered, but never buckled, from the blow.

Afterglow

A dead love leaves a heart, they say,
cold as unyielding stone,
but on a sunlit summer's day
even a stone grows warm.
As the pavement holds the heat
after the sun has died,
so still my heart embraces warmth
though you are not inside.

Lament

Love came dancing lightly
from eyes of laughing blue
and had I read them rightly,
known them to be untrue,
the numbing years that followed,
the heart of heavy stone,
the salty tears I swallowed,
today would be unknown.
The stars still twinkle brightly,
and beckon as of yore,
and love comes dancing lightly.
(I've heard that song before.)

Unanswered

My lips say, "Is it all of ten
years since last we met?
How odd that we should meet again."
cool, calm, polite, and yet,
my heart cries out, *It was ten years*
upon the first of May.
You kissed my eyes abrim with tears
and turned your heart away.

Your lips reply, "Ten years, that's so.
But you are looking fine."
Your heart, as in the long ago,
fails to answer mine.

Glimpses

I have a home and family now
and I am happy—quite.
But sometimes when the moon hangs low
and apple trees show white,
the ashes shift, the cobwebs part
as through a windowpane,
I see a torn and wretched heart
sobbing in the lane.

LAND LOVERS

Before The Storm

Balls of feather cling on brittle claws,
huddled together on a limb for warmth.
The wires are bare. Bird wisdom knows
a wire's swaying perch follows
the wind. Some instinct bids them
trust a trembling tree, although,
I see but little difference.
Perhaps the tree is friendlier to toes.

Eyes dart, seeking the smallest
seed the wind may lift.
For this, a bird would risk
its space upon a limb.

First snow flakes mist to diamonds
on my hair. I catch one perfect star
upon my tongue and stiff cheeks smile.
I do not feel them move, but I feel ice
riding my breath to sear my throat.
I seek the sky and pray for birds as toes
stumble on rutted tracks to take me home.

Wind

The wind has mischief on his mind today.
He tilts the perches of the ruffled birds
and talks to trees in whispered secret words.
There is a sort of madness in his play.
He snatches hats from unsuspecting men
and lifts the skirts of women when they walk.
The geese fly low complaining as they talk,
and fallen leaves attempt to rise again,
He pirouettes with laughter in his tones,
whistles around the corner of a shed,
tortures and shreds the aster's faded bed
and puts a shiver in an old man's bones.
Today is play. I wonder does he know
tomorrow he must heap fresh-fallen snow.

Time of Rebirth

Spring pushes fingers of hope against the skin,
prods optimism out of hibernation; the senses
draw deep inhalations; suddenly the mind
spins summer dreams. There is no living thing
that does not feel rebirth in spring.

March Snow

The snow came boldly yesterday,
riding the wind and stinging faces;
it shoved against a wall, a fence,
and squeezed into the sheltered spaces.

Today it shrinks upon itself,
retreats to shadows in dismay.
The sun came out and called its bluff.
In flowing tears, it runs away.

Conococheague

Conococheague, you catch the morning sun.
No other water sparkles with such glow
as you upon your twinkling surface show
with each new day when it is first begun.
But morning does not boast the only one
to stir your bubbled laughter as you flow;
at twilight I can hear you singing low
your canticle as over stones you run.
The Indian who named you in the past
when fish jumped high, that seldom do today,
surely must have found you in a dream
and brought his tribe to kneel here and to pray
that they had found a welcome home at last
Conococheague—dancing, sacred stream.

Rose Bounty

Come and see my roses
unfold their glory free
in sudden bountiful release,
cascading ecstasy.
Massive bowls of purest cream
overflow the bough.
God has outdone his rosary,
Oh, see my garden now.

Rainbows

Rays of filtered sun
arc heavenward
in sprays of mist,
never quite reaching God
before the colors
climb the clouds to drift,
wistful as a dream,
silently back to earth.

Love Song to the Hills

I am one with the hills
and in me is a mountain.
All my years I fled to hilltops
pouring out my pain.
I beat the earth with fists of rage,
wept out my tears,
pressed the earth until its comfort
filtered through my bones.
With hands of love, I held its blossoms,
shouted my ecstasies to the wind.

It is not strange
that in me is a mountain.
Where I left so much of me,
I took a mountain in, and here
so far away where flat lands stretch,
I lean upon an inner peak for strength.
But O, when time and distance separate
me and my hilltops overlong, I ache
to be united with my other part.
I hear a mountain crying.

Memoriam

There was a quiet road that stretched
mailbox to mailbox through unmeasured time,
all velvet dust in dappled sun and shade.
Trees beckoned each other, arms outstretched,
and whispered secret words above its crown.

I do not recognize its contours now,
ravished beneath cement. Somewhere
below the tons of mounded earth, a road
remembers silence, as I remember birds
that twittered grace for blackberries.

My eyes seek yesterday
beneath the violation of the years.
Some may see a victory for progress.
All I know is peace
was here and is no more.
A sadness breaths in me.

Pollution

I will remember when the earth is bare
how cool, green grass left moisture on my toes.
I will recall, breathing polluted air,
the lilac's perfume drift against my nose.
But O my children's children, yet unborn,
will there be time for you to touch and see,
to smell the wonder of a rain-washed morn,
or will you be too late for memory?

Prologue To The Rockies

Kansas is a preparation. Going west
it grades the memory, levels the lush green
ridges of the east to naked prairie land.
It makes a song of dry winds, effacing streams,
sweeping hot dust into last vestiges
of preconceived ideas.
Only after Kansas, is the mind
prepared to comprehend the stark reality
of sudden pinnacles lifting from the flat bed
of the plains, haughty and imperious,
halfway up to God.

Warm Day in Winter

The birds were frivolous today
pretending it was spring.
They frittered all the day away;
I told them to go home
before the winter caught them north
and froze their foolish throats,
or ice wings bound them to the earth.
Then the warbled notes
reverberated in my soul
and set it winging free,
and there was no one pole-to-pole
who sang so joyfully.

Hay and Pie Cherries

It was July and haying time.
Girls do not pitch hay, but golden shocks
lay cured upon the field and rain was due.

I stood high on the wagon pulling back
the heaps the forks pitched up.
Shoulders flashed pain signals to my wrists
and down my spine, sweat rivulets
were dusted in with chaff. There was no time
to wipe steam from my lashes or to heed
the stinging stalks that slapped bare ankles.

Step up, scoop the lifted sheaves,
step back, avoid the silver prongs.
In rhythm to the swinging tines, I danced
with God up there against the sky.

When the tractor pulled the swaying load
down to the barn we sprawled upon the field,
too worn for thought or speech. Thirst
thickened throats, outweighed fatigue,
and summoning our bones, we limped to where
a tree, laden with fruit, bordered the field.
Now, half a century and miles away,
each time I pass a stubbled field,
I taste pie cherries cool upon my lips
and smell the dusty warmth of new mown hay.

Lois Anderson Leister

Campfire Magic

There is magic in a campfire
when flames leap hot and high;
the kindling sparks and crackles,
and the juices hiss and sigh.

There is magic in a campfire,
whether oak or knot of pine,
to soften up the shoe soles
and the frostbite on your spine.

There is magic in a campfire
when the dark is throbbing low
and lonely at the edges
of the ember's crimson glow.

But the finest campfire magic
is the fellowship it lends
in golden benediction,
to a group of camping friends.

Urgency

My native hills cry out to me
as autumn bends the apple bough.
The maples clad flamboyantly
in red and gold, proclaim a now
that changes momentarily,
extended time does not allow.
My native hills cry out to me
as autumn bends the apple bough.
They bid me from my shackles flee
lest winter frost the mountain's brow
to gray-boned bleak obscurity
before my soul responds to how
my native hills cry out to me
as autumn bends the apple bough.

Ettalong, Australia

I will remember Ettalong
with mountains lifted high,
the steep descending tunnels
and trains that silver by,
and at low tide the oyster beds
left drying in the sun.
I have a wealth of memories,
and treasure every one:
the bell birds, hidden in the trees,
that sang the purest notes,
like bells of finest porcelain
from out of tiny throats.
I will remember Ettalong;
it held me for a day
of warmth and beauty,
sun and sea, before I went away.
I will remember Ettalong
and feel a touch of pain
for good friends that I know and love
and may not see again.

April

The wind has softened, gentled as it blows,
and flooded freshets spray the mountainside,
as from a tight green cup, an early rose
summons the courage up to open wide.

God's paintbrush spreads green velvet on the hills,
a Rembrandt could not duplicate the shade,
and interspersed are golden daffodils,
while violets spread purple in the glade.

The silent ponds awaken giving voice
from lily pads and moss-clad sunken logs.
The frogs have formed a chorus to rejoice
and sing of April to the pollywogs.

This Land

This land is mine. I own its majesty:
the mountains green with pine, the distant sea.
This land is mine and I will tend its seed,
although, by God's design, I have no deed
that gives me claim to this beloved soil.
And yet, I will not maim, I will not spoil
one bit of sod, one creature, or one tree
in all the land that God entrusts to me.

TOMORROW
LAND

Envelopes

A fluttered sigh gathers one last pulse
still harbored in her throat, lifts and is gone.
The envelope that held her dreams flattens
the empty sheet shaped to her bones.
Silence is sound ethereal winding the air;
its promise calls her home.

My soul rises, follows on a sigh,
stretches its tether almost free.
Then I remember thoughts unwritten,
dreams unfinished, paths
untraveled, prayers unspoken.
Floating on a tear, I slip
my soul back into its envelope.

Sounds and Silence

Unexpected silence shouts
and vibrates in the brain.
There is not a person doubts
the screaming of a pain.

There is a roar of agony
before a rush of tears,
and joy can set a memory
to music all your years.

But one night on a mountain wild
it paused then hurried on,
and covering a sleeping child,
it found me in the dawn.

A time of perfect stillness
when even echoes cease,
in momentary gentle hush,
the holiness of peace.

Midnight in the Hospital

I'm going home tomorrow
and I need to sleep tonight,
yet I lie contentedly
awaiting morning light.
My bed is filled beyond capacity
with God and love, my husband,
my new born babe and me.

Lois Anderson Leister

Freedom

Something in me is ever free,
born of the wind on wooded hilltops,
a meadow that no feet have matted,
dark that echoes insect voices.
Beyond the peering glass-eyed windows
something in me is ever aching
to race the wind, to kiss a snowflake,
to feel the stillness saturating.
I must run as though escaping
all that is man-made, every shadow,
and flee into the silence God made.

Aging

My wrapping has grown wrinkled,
my steps are getting slow;
I find myself forgetting
the things that I should know.
But as age overtakes me,
and there's no room for pride.
It gives my poor soul space to grow
with more of God inside.

Final Victory

My soul and body disagree
until they split my brain,
the one is light as laughter,
the other, sodden pain.

My soul, undaunted by a sea,
would spirit me beyond;
my body, heavy as a stone,
would drown me in a pond.

Although I outwardly accept
the boundaries of my skin;
nothing, not even death itself,
shall limit me within.

Benediction

When I must close my life on earth,
let the last sound I hear
be laughter, my last sight
be rain-wet leaves catching the sun,
and my last thought
be *I am ready, Lord.*

Lois Anderson Leister

Sudden Things

Thank you God, for sudden things
that lift me with their glow:
a balmy, out of season day
between two months of snow,
or bird song after singing birds
have sought a warmer nest.
After endless hours of toil,
success and quiet rest.
And in the moments after
dignity falls apart,
thank you, God, for laughter
to lift the foolish heart.

Thank You

I do not know what changed Your mind
or what I did deserving of reward.
I only know the loneliness confined
in me, and heretofore, ignored has been
dispelled. Though they include my thanks,
my prayers are nothing to my gratitude.

My Song

Time is slipping through the sieve
and many I have loved are gone.
But God remembers that I live
and fills my stumbling soul with song.

Beauty

Beauty is the poetry
of earth, the sea, the sky,
a burst of sudden laughter,
a soft warm baby's cry,
the whiteness of a snow field,
the darkness of a hole,
the bright and overflowing cup
of singing in a soul.

A Singing Soul

After loss had filled my years
with bitterness and doubt,
and every memory brought tears,
my soul rose with a shout.

This is not why God put you here,
it told my sodden brain;
the price you pay is far too dear;
stop dwelling in the pain.

I reached, uncertain, for the light,
until God took my hand
to lead me through the bitter night,
and oh, the walk was grand!

Such joy and wonder fill me up;
I cannot hold the whole.
A bright and overflowing cup
of singing fills my soul.

Discovery

God lavishes without a fee,
beauty on a face, a tree,
a country lane, a mountain spire.
But once, imbedded in the mire
of my own ugliness, I learned
inner beauty mst be arndMy
Friendship Wish

May friendships grow
with a golden glow,
and laughter be part
of a loving heart,
and may God fill the whole
of a welcoming soul.

Printed in the United States
60510LVS00003B/163-165

9 781425 955007